50 Russian Pizza Recipes for Home

By: Kelly Johnson

Table of Contents

- Borscht Bliss Pizza
- Pelmeni Pleasure Pizza
- Shashlik Supreme Pizza
- Blini Bonanza Pizza
- Pirozhki Perfection Pizza
- Olivier Extravaganza Pizza
- Kvass Carnival Pizza
- Syrniki Sensation Pizza
- Solyanka Surprise Pizza
- Medovik Magic Pizza
- Zakuski Zest Pizza
- Ukha Elegance Pizza
- Kulebyaka Kiss Pizza
- Okroshka Odyssey Pizza
- Caviar Celebration Pizza
- Vatrushka Velvet Pizza
- Holodets Harmony Pizza
- Kasha Kreation Pizza
- Kvass Kicker Pizza
- Smetana Symphony Pizza
- Tvorog Tango Pizza
- Shuba Supreme Pizza
- Pryaniki Paradise Pizza
- Kompot Kudos Pizza
- Draniki Delight Pizza
- Zefir Zenith Pizza
- Sharlotka Splendor Pizza
- Tula Gingerbread Gourmet Pizza
- Olivier Ovation Pizza
- Sbiten Sensational Pizza
- Grechka Gourmet Pizza
- Uzvar Utopia Pizza
- Syrniki Symphony Pizza
- Ryba Po-Russki Royale Pizza
- Pryanik Pleasure Pizza

- Maslenitsa Marvel Pizza
- Tula Tea Cake Supreme Pizza
- Kulich Kiss Pizza
- Solyanka Splurge Pizza
- Sbiten Spice Pizza
- Zapekanka Zen Pizza
- Zharkoye Zest Pizza
- Tvorog Toast Pizza
- Ukha Utopia Pizza
- Holodets Happiness Pizza
- Kisel Kudos Pizza
- Paskha Perfection Pizza
- Pelmeni Party Pizza
- Sbiten Sensation Pizza
- Vareniki Velvet Pizza

Borscht Bliss Pizza

Ingredients:

- Pizza dough
- 1 cup borscht (beet soup), cooled
- 1/2 cup sour cream
- 1/4 cup red onion, thinly sliced
- 1/4 cup boiled and diced potatoes
- 1/4 cup pickled beets, sliced
- Fresh dill, chopped (for garnish)
- Salt and pepper to taste

Instructions:

Preheat your oven according to the pizza dough instructions.
Roll out the pizza dough on a floured surface to your desired thickness.
Spread a layer of sour cream evenly over the pizza dough.
Pour the cooled borscht over the sour cream layer.
Scatter thinly sliced red onions, boiled and diced potatoes, and pickled beet slices over the borscht.
Season with salt and pepper to taste.
Bake in the preheated oven until the crust is golden, and the toppings are heated through.
Remove from the oven and let it cool for a few minutes.
Garnish with chopped fresh dill.
Slice and serve your Borscht Bliss Pizza, a unique and flavorful twist on the classic Russian beet soup!

Pelmeni Pleasure Pizza

Ingredients:

- Pizza dough
- 1 cup cooked pelmeni (Russian dumplings), cooled
- 1/2 cup sour cream
- 1/4 cup green onions, chopped
- 1/4 cup cooked and crumbled bacon
- 1 cup mozzarella cheese, shredded
- Salt and pepper to taste

Instructions:

Preheat your oven according to the pizza dough instructions.
Roll out the pizza dough on a floured surface to your desired thickness.
Spread a layer of sour cream evenly over the pizza dough.
Distribute the cooked pelmeni over the sour cream layer.
Sprinkle chopped green onions and crumbled bacon over the pelmeni.
Sprinkle shredded mozzarella cheese over the entire pizza.
Season with salt and pepper to taste.
Bake in the preheated oven until the crust is golden, and the cheese is melted and bubbly.
Remove from the oven and let it cool for a few minutes.
Slice and serve your Pelmeni Pleasure Pizza, a delightful fusion of Russian dumplings with the classic pizza experience!

Shashlik Supreme Pizza

Ingredients:

- Pizza dough
- 1 cup shashlik-style marinated meat (beef, pork, or chicken), cooked and sliced
- 1/2 cup bell peppers, sliced
- 1/2 cup red onion, thinly sliced
- 1/4 cup cherry tomatoes, halved
- 1 cup feta cheese, crumbled
- Olive oil (for drizzling)
- Fresh cilantro, chopped (for garnish)
- Salt and pepper to taste

Instructions:

Preheat your oven according to the pizza dough instructions.
Roll out the pizza dough on a floured surface to your desired thickness.
Spread a thin layer of olive oil evenly over the pizza dough.
Arrange the cooked and sliced shashlik-style meat over the pizza.
Scatter sliced bell peppers, thinly sliced red onions, and halved cherry tomatoes over the meat.
Sprinkle crumbled feta cheese over the entire pizza.
Season with salt and pepper to taste.
Bake in the preheated oven until the crust is golden, and the toppings are heated through.
Remove from the oven and let it cool for a few minutes.
Drizzle a little more olive oil over the hot pizza.
Garnish with chopped fresh cilantro.
Slice and serve your Shashlik Supreme Pizza, a delicious fusion of Russian shashlik flavors on a pizza crust!

Blini Bonanza Pizza

Ingredients:

- Pizza dough
- 1 cup blini (Russian pancakes), cooked and cooled
- 1/4 cup sour cream
- 1/4 cup smoked salmon, thinly sliced
- 1/4 cup red onion, finely chopped
- 2 tablespoons capers
- Fresh dill, chopped (for garnish)
- Lemon wedges (for serving)

Instructions:

Preheat your oven according to the pizza dough instructions.
Roll out the pizza dough on a floured surface to your desired thickness.
Spread a layer of sour cream evenly over the pizza dough.
Place the cooked and cooled blini over the sour cream layer.
Arrange thinly sliced smoked salmon over the blini.
Sprinkle finely chopped red onion and capers over the salmon.
Bake in the preheated oven until the crust is golden, and the toppings are heated through.
Remove from the oven and let it cool for a few minutes.
Garnish with chopped fresh dill.
Serve with lemon wedges on the side for added flavor.
Slice and enjoy your Blini Bonanza Pizza, a delightful blend of Russian blini with the classic pizza experience!

Pirozhki Perfection Pizza

Ingredients:

- Pizza dough
- 1 cup pirozhki filling (ground meat, cabbage, or potato), cooked and cooled
- 1/4 cup Russian mustard
- 1/4 cup dill pickles, diced
- 1 cup cheddar cheese, shredded
- Fresh parsley, chopped (for garnish)
- Salt and pepper to taste

Instructions:

Preheat your oven according to the pizza dough instructions.
Roll out the pizza dough on a floured surface to your desired thickness.
Spread a layer of Russian mustard evenly over the pizza dough.
Distribute the cooked and cooled pirozhki filling over the mustard layer.
Scatter diced dill pickles over the filling.
Sprinkle shredded cheddar cheese over the entire pizza.
Season with salt and pepper to taste.
Bake in the preheated oven until the crust is golden, and the cheese is melted and bubbly.
Remove from the oven and let it cool for a few minutes.
Garnish with chopped fresh parsley.
Slice and serve your Pirozhki Perfection Pizza, a delicious blend of Russian pirozhki flavors on a pizza crust!

Olivier Extravaganza Pizza

Ingredients:

- Pizza dough
- 1 cup Olivier salad, chilled
- 1/4 cup mayonnaise
- 1/4 cup ham, diced
- 1/4 cup cooked peas
- 1/4 cup carrots, finely diced
- 1/4 cup pickles, finely diced
- 1/4 cup boiled potatoes, diced
- 1 cup mozzarella cheese, shredded
- Fresh parsley, chopped (for garnish)
- Salt and pepper to taste

Instructions:

Preheat your oven according to the pizza dough instructions.
Roll out the pizza dough on a floured surface to your desired thickness.
In a bowl, mix together the Olivier salad, mayonnaise, diced ham, cooked peas, finely diced carrots, finely diced pickles, and diced boiled potatoes.
Spread the Olivier salad mixture evenly over the pizza dough.
Sprinkle shredded mozzarella cheese over the entire pizza.
Season with salt and pepper to taste.
Bake in the preheated oven until the crust is golden, and the cheese is melted and bubbly.
Remove from the oven and let it cool for a few minutes.
Garnish with chopped fresh parsley.
Slice and serve your Olivier Extravaganza Pizza, a delightful twist on the classic Russian Olivier salad presented on a pizza crust!

Kvass Carnival Pizza

Ingredients:

- Pizza dough
- 1 cup kvass-infused sauce (tomato-based with kvass)
- 1/2 cup smoked sausage, sliced
- 1/4 cup red bell pepper, thinly sliced
- 1/4 cup green bell pepper, thinly sliced
- 1/4 cup onions, thinly sliced
- 1 cup gouda cheese, shredded
- Fresh chives, chopped (for garnish)
- Olive oil (for drizzling)
- Salt and pepper to taste

Instructions:

Preheat your oven according to the pizza dough instructions.
Roll out the pizza dough on a floured surface to your desired thickness.
Spread a layer of the kvass-infused sauce evenly over the pizza dough.
Distribute sliced smoked sausage over the sauce.
Scatter thinly sliced red and green bell peppers, and onions over the sausage.
Sprinkle shredded gouda cheese over the entire pizza.
Season with salt and pepper to taste.
Bake in the preheated oven until the crust is golden, and the cheese is melted and bubbly.
Remove from the oven and let it cool for a few minutes.
Drizzle a little olive oil over the hot pizza.
Garnish with chopped fresh chives.
Slice and serve your Kvass Carnival Pizza, a flavorful pizza celebrating the Russian drink kvass with a carnival of delicious toppings!

Syrniki Sensation Pizza

Ingredients:

- Pizza dough
- 1 cup syrniki (Russian cottage cheese pancakes), crumbled
- 1/4 cup sour cream
- 1/4 cup raspberry jam
- 1/4 cup fresh berries (such as blueberries or raspberries)
- 1/4 cup slivered almonds
- Powdered sugar (for dusting)
- Mint leaves (for garnish)

Instructions:

Preheat your oven according to the pizza dough instructions.
Roll out the pizza dough on a floured surface to your desired thickness.
Spread a layer of sour cream evenly over the pizza dough.
Distribute crumbled syrniki over the sour cream layer.
Drizzle raspberry jam over the syrniki.
Scatter fresh berries and slivered almonds over the entire pizza.
Bake in the preheated oven until the crust is golden, and the toppings are heated through.
Remove from the oven and let it cool for a few minutes.
Dust with powdered sugar for added sweetness.
Garnish with mint leaves.
Slice and serve your Syrniki Sensation Pizza, a delightful blend of Russian cottage cheese pancakes with a sweet and fruity twist on a pizza!

Solyanka Surprise Pizza

Ingredients:

- Pizza dough
- 1 cup solyanka soup base, cooked and drained
- 1/2 cup mixed cured meats (such as sausage, ham, and salami), sliced
- 1/4 cup pickles, sliced
- 1/4 cup black olives, sliced
- 1 cup mozzarella cheese, shredded
- Fresh dill, chopped (for garnish)
- Lemon wedges (for serving)

Instructions:

Preheat your oven according to the pizza dough instructions.
Roll out the pizza dough on a floured surface to your desired thickness.
Spread a layer of the cooked and drained solyanka soup base evenly over the pizza dough.
Arrange slices of mixed cured meats over the solyanka.
Scatter sliced pickles and black olives over the meats.
Sprinkle shredded mozzarella cheese over the entire pizza.
Bake in the preheated oven until the crust is golden, and the cheese is melted and bubbly.
Remove from the oven and let it cool for a few minutes.
Garnish with chopped fresh dill.
Serve with lemon wedges on the side for added flavor.
Slice and enjoy your Solyanka Surprise Pizza, a surprising and savory twist inspired by the Russian solyanka soup!

Medovik Magic Pizza

Ingredients:

- Pizza dough
- 1 cup honey cake filling (honey, sour cream, and crushed cookies), mixed
- 1/4 cup walnuts, chopped
- 1/4 cup chocolate chips
- 1/4 cup whipped cream
- Honey (for drizzling)
- Edible flowers (for garnish)

Instructions:

Preheat your oven according to the pizza dough instructions.
Roll out the pizza dough on a floured surface to your desired thickness.
Spread the honey cake filling evenly over the pizza dough.
Sprinkle chopped walnuts and chocolate chips over the honey cake filling.
Bake in the preheated oven until the crust is golden and cooked through.
Remove from the oven and let it cool for a few minutes.
Drizzle honey over the hot pizza.
Dollop whipped cream on top.
Garnish with edible flowers.
Slice and serve your Medovik Magic Pizza, a sweet and delightful fusion of pizza and the Russian honey cake, Medovik!

Zakuski Zest Pizza

Ingredients:

- Pizza dough
- 1 cup zakuski-inspired toppings (pickled vegetables, marinated mushrooms, herring, and Russian-style pickles), chopped
- 1/4 cup mayonnaise
- 1/4 cup fresh dill, chopped
- 1/4 cup red onion, thinly sliced
- 1 cup Russian cheese blend (or a mix of Swiss and Gouda), shredded
- Lemon wedges (for serving)

Instructions:

Preheat your oven according to the pizza dough instructions.
Roll out the pizza dough on a floured surface to your desired thickness.
Spread a layer of mayonnaise evenly over the pizza dough.
Distribute the zakuski-inspired toppings over the mayonnaise layer.
Sprinkle chopped fresh dill and thinly sliced red onions over the toppings.
Sprinkle the Russian cheese blend (or Swiss and Gouda mix) over the entire pizza.
Bake in the preheated oven until the crust is golden, and the cheese is melted and bubbly.
Remove from the oven and let it cool for a few minutes.
Serve with lemon wedges on the side for added zing.
Slice and savor your Zakuski Zest Pizza, a flavorful and appetizing pizza inspired by Russian zakuski appetizers!

Ukha Elegance Pizza

Ingredients:

- Pizza dough
- 1 cup ukha-inspired toppings (salmon, white fish, vegetables), cooked and flaked
- 1/4 cup sour cream
- 1/4 cup leeks, finely sliced
- 1/4 cup fresh dill, chopped
- 1/4 cup cherry tomatoes, halved
- 1 cup mozzarella cheese, shredded
- Lemon wedges (for serving)

Instructions:

Preheat your oven according to the pizza dough instructions.
Roll out the pizza dough on a floured surface to your desired thickness.
Spread a layer of sour cream evenly over the pizza dough.
Distribute the ukha-inspired toppings (cooked and flaked salmon, white fish, and vegetables) over the sour cream layer.
Sprinkle finely sliced leeks, chopped fresh dill, and halved cherry tomatoes over the toppings.
Sprinkle shredded mozzarella cheese over the entire pizza.
Bake in the preheated oven until the crust is golden, and the cheese is melted and bubbly.
Remove from the oven and let it cool for a few minutes.
Serve with lemon wedges on the side for a citrusy touch.
Slice and relish your Ukha Elegance Pizza, a sophisticated and flavorful pizza inspired by the Russian fish soup, ukha!

Kulebyaka Kiss Pizza

Ingredients:

- Pizza dough
- 1 cup kulebyaka-inspired filling (salmon, rice, mushrooms), cooked and cooled
- 1/4 cup puff pastry, crumbled
- 1/4 cup cream cheese
- 1/4 cup green onions, chopped
- 1 cup Swiss cheese, shredded
- Fresh dill, chopped (for garnish)
- Lemon wedges (for serving)

Instructions:

Preheat your oven according to the pizza dough instructions.
Roll out the pizza dough on a floured surface to your desired thickness.
Spread a layer of cream cheese evenly over the pizza dough.
Distribute the kulebyaka-inspired filling (cooked salmon, rice, and mushrooms) over the cream cheese layer.
Sprinkle crumbled puff pastry and chopped green onions over the filling.
Sprinkle shredded Swiss cheese over the entire pizza.
Bake in the preheated oven until the crust is golden, and the cheese is melted and bubbly.
Remove from the oven and let it cool for a few minutes.
Garnish with chopped fresh dill.
Serve with lemon wedges on the side for a citrusy accent.
Slice and enjoy your Kulebyaka Kiss Pizza, a delectable pizza inspired by the Russian pastry dish, kulebyaka!

Okroshka Odyssey Pizza

Ingredients:

- Pizza dough
- 1 cup okroshka-inspired toppings (cucumbers, radishes, boiled eggs), finely chopped
- 1/4 cup kefir or yogurt
- 1/4 cup mayonnaise
- 1/4 cup fresh dill, chopped
- 1/4 cup green onions, thinly sliced
- 1 cup feta cheese, crumbled
- Salt and pepper to taste

Instructions:

Preheat your oven according to the pizza dough instructions.
Roll out the pizza dough on a floured surface to your desired thickness.
In a bowl, mix together kefir (or yogurt) and mayonnaise to create a creamy base.
Spread the creamy mixture evenly over the pizza dough.
Distribute the okroshka-inspired toppings (finely chopped cucumbers, radishes, and boiled eggs) over the creamy base.
Sprinkle chopped fresh dill and thinly sliced green onions over the toppings.
Crumble feta cheese over the entire pizza.
Season with salt and pepper to taste.
Bake in the preheated oven until the crust is golden, and the toppings are fresh and flavorful.
Remove from the oven and let it cool for a few minutes.
Slice and savor your Okroshka Odyssey Pizza, a refreshing and unique pizza inspired by the Russian cold soup, okroshka!

Caviar Celebration Pizza

Ingredients:

- Pizza dough
- 1/4 cup crème fraîche or sour cream
- 1/4 cup red onion, finely chopped
- 2 tablespoons chives, finely chopped
- 1/4 cup smoked salmon, thinly sliced
- 2 tablespoons black caviar
- 1 tablespoon capers
- Lemon wedges (for serving)

Instructions:

Preheat your oven according to the pizza dough instructions.
Roll out the pizza dough on a floured surface to your desired thickness.
Spread a layer of crème fraîche or sour cream evenly over the pizza dough.
Sprinkle finely chopped red onion and chives over the cream layer.
Arrange thinly sliced smoked salmon on top.
Place dollops of black caviar evenly over the pizza.
Scatter capers over the caviar.
Bake in the preheated oven until the crust is golden, and the toppings are just heated through.
Remove from the oven and let it cool for a few minutes.
Serve with lemon wedges on the side for a citrusy touch.
Slice and enjoy your Caviar Celebration Pizza, a luxurious and elegant pizza inspired by the opulence of caviar!

Vatrushka Velvet Pizza

Ingredients:

- Pizza dough
- 1 cup tvorog (Russian farmer's cheese or cottage cheese)
- 1/4 cup sugar
- 1 egg
- 1/4 cup raisins
- 1/4 cup apricot jam
- 1/4 cup heavy cream
- 1 teaspoon vanilla extract
- Powdered sugar (for dusting)
- Fresh mint leaves (for garnish)

Instructions:

Preheat your oven according to the pizza dough instructions.
Roll out the pizza dough on a floured surface to your desired thickness.
In a bowl, combine tvorog (farmer's cheese or cottage cheese), sugar, egg, raisins, apricot jam, heavy cream, and vanilla extract. Mix well to create the sweet cheese filling.
Spread the sweet cheese filling evenly over the pizza dough.
Bake in the preheated oven until the crust is golden and the cheese filling is set.
Remove from the oven and let it cool for a few minutes.
Dust with powdered sugar for added sweetness.
Garnish with fresh mint leaves.
Slice and serve your Vatrushka Velvet Pizza, a delightful and sweet pizza inspired by the traditional Russian pastry, vatrushka!

Holodets Harmony Pizza

Ingredients:

- Pizza dough
- 1 cup holodets-inspired toppings (gelatinous meat aspic, diced)
- 1/4 cup horseradish sauce
- 1/4 cup red onion, thinly sliced
- 1/4 cup fresh parsley, chopped
- 1/4 cup pickles, finely diced
- 1 cup provolone cheese, shredded
- Salt and pepper to taste

Instructions:

Preheat your oven according to the pizza dough instructions.
Roll out the pizza dough on a floured surface to your desired thickness.
Spread a layer of horseradish sauce evenly over the pizza dough.
Distribute the holodets-inspired toppings (gelatinous meat aspic, diced) over the horseradish layer.
Scatter thinly sliced red onion, chopped fresh parsley, and finely diced pickles over the toppings.
Sprinkle shredded provolone cheese over the entire pizza.
Season with salt and pepper to taste.
Bake in the preheated oven until the crust is golden, and the cheese is melted and bubbly.
Remove from the oven and let it cool for a few minutes.
Slice and enjoy your Holodets Harmony Pizza, a unique and savory pizza inspired by the Russian meat jelly, holodets!

Kasha Kreation Pizza

Ingredients:

- Pizza dough
- 1 cup kasha (buckwheat groats), cooked
- 1/4 cup caramelized onions
- 1/4 cup mushrooms, sliced
- 1/4 cup goat cheese, crumbled
- 1/4 cup fresh thyme leaves
- Olive oil (for drizzling)
- Salt and pepper to taste

Instructions:

Preheat your oven according to the pizza dough instructions.
Roll out the pizza dough on a floured surface to your desired thickness.
Spread the cooked kasha evenly over the pizza dough.
Distribute caramelized onions and sliced mushrooms over the kasha.
Sprinkle crumbled goat cheese over the entire pizza.
Sprinkle fresh thyme leaves over the toppings.
Drizzle a little olive oil over the pizza.
Season with salt and pepper to taste.
Bake in the preheated oven until the crust is golden, and the toppings are heated through.
Remove from the oven and let it cool for a few minutes.
Slice and savor your Kasha Kreation Pizza, a creative and wholesome pizza inspired by Russian buckwheat groats!

Kvass Kicker Pizza

Ingredients:

- Pizza dough
- 1 cup kvass-infused tomato sauce
- 1/4 cup sausage, crumbled
- 1/4 cup bell peppers, thinly sliced
- 1/4 cup red onion, diced
- 1/4 cup pickles, sliced
- 1 cup cheddar cheese, shredded
- Fresh dill, chopped (for garnish)
- Olive oil (for drizzling)
- Salt and pepper to taste

Instructions:

Preheat your oven according to the pizza dough instructions.
Roll out the pizza dough on a floured surface to your desired thickness.
Spread a layer of the kvass-infused tomato sauce evenly over the pizza dough.
Sprinkle crumbled sausage, thinly sliced bell peppers, diced red onion, and sliced pickles over the sauce.
Sprinkle shredded cheddar cheese over the entire pizza.
Season with salt and pepper to taste.
Bake in the preheated oven until the crust is golden, and the cheese is melted and bubbly.
Remove from the oven and let it cool for a few minutes.
Drizzle a little olive oil over the hot pizza.
Garnish with chopped fresh dill.
Slice and enjoy your Kvass Kicker Pizza, a flavorful pizza inspired by the Russian beverage, kvass!

Smetana Symphony Pizza

Ingredients:

- Pizza dough
- 1/2 cup smetana (sour cream)
- 1/4 cup cooked and shredded chicken
- 1/4 cup red onion, thinly sliced
- 1/4 cup cucumber, thinly sliced
- 1/4 cup cherry tomatoes, halved
- 1/4 cup fresh dill, chopped
- 1 cup mozzarella cheese, shredded
- Salt and pepper to taste

Instructions:

Preheat your oven according to the pizza dough instructions.
Roll out the pizza dough on a floured surface to your desired thickness.
Spread a layer of smetana (sour cream) evenly over the pizza dough.
Distribute the shredded chicken over the sour cream layer.
Scatter thinly sliced red onion, cucumber slices, and halved cherry tomatoes over the chicken.
Sprinkle chopped fresh dill over the toppings.
Sprinkle shredded mozzarella cheese over the entire pizza.
Season with salt and pepper to taste.
Bake in the preheated oven until the crust is golden, and the cheese is melted and bubbly.
Remove from the oven and let it cool for a few minutes.
Slice and savor your Smetana Symphony Pizza, a harmonious blend of flavors inspired by the Russian sour cream, smetana!

Tvorog Tango Pizza

Ingredients:

- Pizza dough
- 1 cup tvorog (Russian farmer's cheese or cottage cheese)
- 1/4 cup sugar
- 1 egg
- 1/4 cup raisins
- 1/4 cup apricot jam
- 1/4 cup walnuts, chopped
- Powdered sugar (for dusting)
- Fresh mint leaves (for garnish)

Instructions:

Preheat your oven according to the pizza dough instructions.
Roll out the pizza dough on a floured surface to your desired thickness.
In a bowl, combine tvorog (farmer's cheese or cottage cheese), sugar, egg, raisins, apricot jam, and chopped walnuts. Mix well to create the sweet cheese filling.
Spread the sweet cheese filling evenly over the pizza dough.
Bake in the preheated oven until the crust is golden and the cheese filling is set.
Remove from the oven and let it cool for a few minutes.
Dust with powdered sugar for added sweetness.
Garnish with fresh mint leaves.
Slice and serve your Tvorog Tango Pizza, a delightful and sweet pizza inspired by the traditional Russian farmer's cheese, tvorog!

Shuba Supreme Pizza

Ingredients:

- Pizza dough
- 1/4 cup mayonnaise
- 1/4 cup sour cream
- 1/4 cup pickled herring, finely chopped
- 1/4 cup boiled potatoes, grated
- 1/4 cup boiled carrots, grated
- 1/4 cup beetroot, boiled and grated
- 1/4 cup green onions, thinly sliced
- 1 tablespoon capers
- Salt and pepper to taste

Instructions:

Preheat your oven according to the pizza dough instructions.
Roll out the pizza dough on a floured surface to your desired thickness.
In a bowl, mix together mayonnaise and sour cream to create a creamy base.
Spread the creamy mixture evenly over the pizza dough.
Evenly distribute the finely chopped pickled herring over the creamy base.
Scatter grated boiled potatoes, carrots, and beetroot over the herring.
Sprinkle thinly sliced green onions and capers over the toppings.
Season with salt and pepper to taste.
Bake in the preheated oven until the crust is golden, and the toppings are heated through.
Remove from the oven and let it cool for a few minutes.
Slice and enjoy your Shuba Supreme Pizza, a unique and flavorful pizza inspired by the Russian layered salad, shuba!

Pryaniki Paradise Pizza

Ingredients:

- Pizza dough
- 1/2 cup pryaniki crumbs (Russian spiced honey cookies), crushed
- 1/4 cup honey
- 1/4 cup cream cheese
- 1/4 cup powdered sugar
- 1/4 cup walnuts, chopped
- 1/4 cup dried fruits (apricots, raisins), chopped
- 1/4 cup chocolate chips
- Powdered sugar (for dusting)

Instructions:

Preheat your oven according to the pizza dough instructions.
Roll out the pizza dough on a floured surface to your desired thickness.
In a bowl, mix together honey, cream cheese, and powdered sugar to create a creamy base.
Spread the creamy mixture evenly over the pizza dough.
Sprinkle crushed pryaniki crumbs over the creamy base.
Evenly distribute chopped walnuts, dried fruits, and chocolate chips over the pryaniki crumbs.
Bake in the preheated oven until the crust is golden and the toppings are heated through.
Remove from the oven and let it cool for a few minutes.
Dust with powdered sugar for added sweetness.
Slice and savor your Pryaniki Paradise Pizza, a sweet and spiced pizza inspired by the Russian pryaniki cookies!

Kompot Kudos Pizza

Ingredients:

- Pizza dough
- 1 cup kompot-infused fruit sauce (cooked and blended mixed fruits with sugar and water)
- 1/4 cup fresh berries (such as strawberries, blueberries, and raspberries)
- 1/4 cup peach slices
- 1/4 cup kiwi, sliced
- 1/4 cup mint leaves, chopped
- 1/4 cup powdered sugar (for dusting)

Instructions:

Preheat your oven according to the pizza dough instructions.
Roll out the pizza dough on a floured surface to your desired thickness.
Spread a layer of the kompot-infused fruit sauce evenly over the pizza dough.
Arrange fresh berries, peach slices, and kiwi slices over the fruit sauce.
Sprinkle chopped mint leaves over the toppings.
Bake in the preheated oven until the crust is golden, and the toppings are heated through.
Remove from the oven and let it cool for a few minutes.
Dust with powdered sugar for added sweetness.
Slice and enjoy your Kompot Kudos Pizza, a fruity and refreshing pizza inspired by the Russian fruit drink, kompot!

Draniki Delight Pizza

Ingredients:

- Pizza dough
- 1 cup draniki (potato pancakes), shredded
- 1/4 cup sour cream
- 1/4 cup smoked salmon, thinly sliced
- 1/4 cup red onion, finely chopped
- 1/4 cup chives, chopped
- 1/4 cup cream cheese
- 1 tablespoon capers
- Lemon wedges (for serving)

Instructions:

Preheat your oven according to the pizza dough instructions.
Roll out the pizza dough on a floured surface to your desired thickness.
In a bowl, mix together shredded draniki and sour cream.
Spread the draniki mixture evenly over the pizza dough.
Evenly distribute thinly sliced smoked salmon and finely chopped red onion over the draniki layer.
Dot the pizza with small spoonfuls of cream cheese.
Sprinkle chopped chives and capers over the toppings.
Bake in the preheated oven until the crust is golden, and the toppings are heated through.
Remove from the oven and let it cool for a few minutes.
Serve with lemon wedges on the side for a citrusy touch.
Slice and enjoy your Draniki Delight Pizza, a savory and delightful pizza inspired by the Russian potato pancakes, draniki!

Zefir Zenith Pizza

Ingredients:

- Pizza dough
- 1 cup zefir (Russian marshmallow-like confection), chopped
- 1/4 cup chocolate spread or ganache
- 1/4 cup strawberries, sliced
- 1/4 cup kiwi, sliced
- 1/4 cup shredded coconut
- 1/4 cup powdered sugar (for dusting)
- Mint leaves (for garnish)

Instructions:

Preheat your oven according to the pizza dough instructions.
Roll out the pizza dough on a floured surface to your desired thickness.
Spread a layer of chocolate spread or ganache evenly over the pizza dough.
Evenly distribute chopped zefir over the chocolate layer.
Arrange sliced strawberries and kiwi over the zefir.
Sprinkle shredded coconut over the toppings.
Bake in the preheated oven until the crust is golden, and the toppings are just heated through.
Remove from the oven and let it cool for a few minutes.
Dust with powdered sugar for added sweetness.
Garnish with mint leaves.
Slice and enjoy your Zefir Zenith Pizza, a sweet and fluffy dessert pizza inspired by the Russian confection, zefir!

Sharlotka Splendor Pizza

Ingredients:

- Pizza dough
- 1 cup sharlotka-inspired apple filling (cooked apples with sugar and cinnamon)
- 1/4 cup caramel sauce
- 1/4 cup walnuts, chopped
- 1/4 cup raisins
- 1/4 cup whipped cream
- Powdered sugar (for dusting)

Instructions:

Preheat your oven according to the pizza dough instructions.
Roll out the pizza dough on a floured surface to your desired thickness.
Spread the sharlotka-inspired apple filling evenly over the pizza dough.
Drizzle caramel sauce over the apple filling.
Evenly distribute chopped walnuts and raisins over the toppings.
Bake in the preheated oven until the crust is golden and the toppings are heated through.
Remove from the oven and let it cool for a few minutes.
Dollop whipped cream on top.
Dust with powdered sugar for added sweetness.
Slice and enjoy your Sharlotka Splendor Pizza, a delicious dessert pizza inspired by the classic Russian apple cake, sharlotka!

Tula Gingerbread Gourmet Pizza

Ingredients:

- Pizza dough
- 1/4 cup honey
- 1/4 cup butter, melted
- 1/4 cup brown sugar
- 1 teaspoon ground cinnamon
- 1/2 teaspoon ground ginger
- 1/4 teaspoon ground cloves
- 1/4 teaspoon baking soda
- 1 cup all-purpose flour
- 1/4 cup powdered sugar (for dusting)
- Whipped cream (for serving)

Instructions:

Preheat your oven according to the pizza dough instructions.
In a bowl, mix together honey, melted butter, brown sugar, ground cinnamon, ground ginger, ground cloves, baking soda, and all-purpose flour. This will form the gingerbread dough.
Roll out the pizza dough on a floured surface to your desired thickness.
Spread the gingerbread dough evenly over the pizza dough.
Bake in the preheated oven until the crust is golden and the gingerbread layer is cooked.
Remove from the oven and let it cool for a few minutes.
Dust with powdered sugar for added sweetness.
Slice and serve with a dollop of whipped cream on top.
Enjoy your Tula Gingerbread Gourmet Pizza, a delightful dessert pizza inspired by the famous Tula gingerbread from Russia!

Olivier Ovation Pizza

Ingredients:

- Pizza dough
- 1/4 cup mayonnaise
- 1/4 cup sour cream
- 1/4 cup cooked and diced potatoes
- 1/4 cup cooked and diced carrots
- 1/4 cup cooked and diced ham
- 1/4 cup cooked and diced peas
- 1/4 cup cooked and diced pickles
- 1/4 cup cooked and diced boiled eggs
- Salt and pepper to taste
- Fresh parsley, chopped (for garnish)

Instructions:

Preheat your oven according to the pizza dough instructions.
Roll out the pizza dough on a floured surface to your desired thickness.
In a bowl, mix together mayonnaise and sour cream to create a creamy base.
Spread the creamy mixture evenly over the pizza dough.
Evenly distribute diced potatoes, carrots, ham, peas, pickles, and boiled eggs over the creamy base.
Season with salt and pepper to taste.
Bake in the preheated oven until the crust is golden, and the toppings are heated through.
Remove from the oven and let it cool for a few minutes.
Garnish with chopped fresh parsley.
Slice and enjoy your Olivier Ovation Pizza, a flavorful pizza inspired by the Russian salad, Olivier!

Sbiten Sensational Pizza

Ingredients:

- Pizza dough
- 1/2 cup sbiten syrup (honey-based Russian spiced drink)
- 1/4 cup cream cheese
- 1/4 cup walnuts, chopped
- 1/4 cup dried fruits (apricots, raisins), chopped
- 1/4 cup apple slices
- 1/4 teaspoon ground cinnamon
- Powdered sugar (for dusting)

Instructions:

Preheat your oven according to the pizza dough instructions.
Roll out the pizza dough on a floured surface to your desired thickness.
Spread a layer of cream cheese evenly over the pizza dough.
Pour sbiten syrup over the cream cheese layer, spreading it evenly.
Evenly distribute chopped walnuts, dried fruits, and apple slices over the toppings.
Sprinkle ground cinnamon over the entire pizza.
Bake in the preheated oven until the crust is golden, and the toppings are heated through.
Remove from the oven and let it cool for a few minutes.
Dust with powdered sugar for added sweetness.
Slice and enjoy your Sbiten Sensational Pizza, a unique and spiced pizza inspired by the traditional Russian drink, sbiten!

Grechka Gourmet Pizza

Ingredients:

- Pizza dough
- 1 cup cooked grechka (buckwheat groats)
- 1/4 cup caramelized onions
- 1/4 cup sautéed mushrooms
- 1/4 cup feta cheese, crumbled
- 1/4 cup spinach leaves
- 1/4 cup roasted cherry tomatoes
- Olive oil (for drizzling)
- Salt and pepper to taste

Instructions:

Preheat your oven according to the pizza dough instructions.
Roll out the pizza dough on a floured surface to your desired thickness.
Spread the cooked grechka (buckwheat groats) evenly over the pizza dough.
Evenly distribute caramelized onions and sautéed mushrooms over the grechka.
Sprinkle crumbled feta cheese over the toppings.
Scatter fresh spinach leaves and roasted cherry tomatoes over the pizza.
Drizzle a little olive oil over the top.
Season with salt and pepper to taste.
Bake in the preheated oven until the crust is golden, and the toppings are heated through.
Remove from the oven and let it cool for a few minutes.
Slice and savor your Grechka Gourmet Pizza, a wholesome and unique pizza inspired by Russian buckwheat groats, grechka!

Uzvar Utopia Pizza

Ingredients:

- Pizza dough
- 1 cup uzvar compote (mixed dried fruits and berries cooked with sugar and water)
- 1/4 cup cream cheese
- 1/4 cup honey
- 1/4 cup mixed nuts (walnuts, almonds, pistachios), chopped
- 1/4 cup pomegranate seeds
- Mint leaves (for garnish)

Instructions:

Preheat your oven according to the pizza dough instructions.
Roll out the pizza dough on a floured surface to your desired thickness.
Spread a layer of cream cheese evenly over the pizza dough.
Pour uzvar compote over the cream cheese layer, spreading it evenly.
Drizzle honey over the compote.
Evenly distribute chopped mixed nuts and pomegranate seeds over the toppings.
Bake in the preheated oven until the crust is golden, and the toppings are heated through.
Remove from the oven and let it cool for a few minutes.
Garnish with fresh mint leaves.
Slice and enjoy your Uzvar Utopia Pizza, a delightful and fruity pizza inspired by the traditional Ukrainian compote, uzvar!

Syrniki Symphony Pizza

Ingredients:

- Pizza dough
- 1 cup syrniki (Russian cottage cheese pancakes), crumbled
- 1/4 cup honey
- 1/4 cup cream cheese
- 1/4 cup fresh berries (strawberries, blueberries, raspberries)
- 1/4 cup chopped nuts (walnuts, almonds)
- Powdered sugar (for dusting)
- Mint leaves (for garnish)

Instructions:

Preheat your oven according to the pizza dough instructions.
Roll out the pizza dough on a floured surface to your desired thickness.
In a bowl, mix crumbled syrniki with honey.
Spread cream cheese evenly over the pizza dough.
Spread the syrniki and honey mixture over the cream cheese layer.
Evenly distribute fresh berries and chopped nuts over the toppings.
Bake in the preheated oven until the crust is golden, and the toppings are just heated through.
Remove from the oven and let it cool for a few minutes.
Dust with powdered sugar for added sweetness.
Garnish with fresh mint leaves.
Slice and enjoy your Syrniki Symphony Pizza, a sweet and creamy pizza inspired by the Russian cottage cheese pancakes, syrniki!

Ryba Po-Russki Royale Pizza

Ingredients:

- Pizza dough
- 1/4 cup mayonnaise
- 1/4 cup sour cream
- 1/4 cup tomato paste
- 1/4 cup red onion, thinly sliced
- 1/4 cup dill pickles, sliced
- 1/4 cup boiled potatoes, sliced
- 1/4 cup boiled carrots, sliced
- 1/4 cup cooked and flaked white fish (cod or haddock)
- 1/4 cup green peas, cooked
- 1/4 teaspoon black pepper
- Fresh dill, chopped (for garnish)

Instructions:

Preheat your oven according to the pizza dough instructions.
Roll out the pizza dough on a floured surface to your desired thickness.
In a bowl, mix together mayonnaise, sour cream, and tomato paste to create a creamy base.
Spread the creamy mixture evenly over the pizza dough.
Evenly distribute thinly sliced red onion, dill pickles, sliced boiled potatoes, sliced boiled carrots, flaked white fish, and cooked green peas over the creamy base.
Sprinkle black pepper over the toppings.
Bake in the preheated oven until the crust is golden, and the toppings are heated through.
Remove from the oven and let it cool for a few minutes.
Garnish with chopped fresh dill.
Slice and enjoy your Ryba Po-Russki Royale Pizza, a seafood-inspired pizza with Russian flavors!

Pryanik Pleasure Pizza

Ingredients:

- Pizza dough
- 1/2 cup pryaniki crumbs (Russian spiced honey cookies), crushed
- 1/4 cup honey
- 1/4 cup cream cheese
- 1/4 cup walnuts, chopped
- 1/4 cup dried fruits (apricots, raisins), chopped
- 1/4 cup chocolate chips
- Powdered sugar (for dusting)

Instructions:

Preheat your oven according to the pizza dough instructions.
Roll out the pizza dough on a floured surface to your desired thickness.
In a bowl, mix together honey, cream cheese, and powdered sugar to create a creamy base.
Spread the creamy mixture evenly over the pizza dough.
Sprinkle crushed pryaniki crumbs over the creamy base.
Evenly distribute chopped walnuts, dried fruits, and chocolate chips over the toppings.
Bake in the preheated oven until the crust is golden, and the toppings are just heated through.
Remove from the oven and let it cool for a few minutes.
Dust with powdered sugar for added sweetness.
Slice and savor your Pryanik Pleasure Pizza, a sweet and spiced pizza inspired by the Russian pryaniki cookies!

Maslenitsa Marvel Pizza

Ingredients:

- Pizza dough
- 1/4 cup melted butter
- 1/4 cup sour cream
- 1/4 cup honey
- 1/4 cup cottage cheese or tvorog
- 1/4 cup strawberries, sliced
- 1/4 cup blueberries
- 1/4 cup powdered sugar (for dusting)
- Fresh mint leaves (for garnish)

Instructions:

Preheat your oven according to the pizza dough instructions.
Roll out the pizza dough on a floured surface to your desired thickness.
In a bowl, mix together melted butter, sour cream, honey, and cottage cheese (or tvorog) to create a creamy base.
Spread the creamy mixture evenly over the pizza dough.
Arrange sliced strawberries and blueberries over the creamy base.
Bake in the preheated oven until the crust is golden, and the toppings are just heated through.
Remove from the oven and let it cool for a few minutes.
Dust with powdered sugar for added sweetness.
Garnish with fresh mint leaves.
Slice and enjoy your Maslenitsa Marvel Pizza, a delightful and sweet pizza inspired by the Russian festival, Maslenitsa!

Tula Tea Cake Supreme Pizza

Ingredients:

- Pizza dough
- 1/2 cup Tula tea cake crumbs (Tula gingerbread or any spiced tea cake), crushed
- 1/4 cup honey
- 1/4 cup cream cheese
- 1/4 cup apple slices
- 1/4 cup caramel sauce
- 1/4 cup chopped nuts (walnuts, almonds)
- Powdered sugar (for dusting)

Instructions:

Preheat your oven according to the pizza dough instructions.
Roll out the pizza dough on a floured surface to your desired thickness.
In a bowl, mix together honey, cream cheese, and powdered sugar to create a creamy base.
Spread the creamy mixture evenly over the pizza dough.
Sprinkle crushed Tula tea cake crumbs over the creamy base.
Arrange apple slices over the tea cake crumbs.
Drizzle caramel sauce over the toppings.
Evenly distribute chopped nuts over the pizza.
Bake in the preheated oven until the crust is golden, and the toppings are just heated through.
Remove from the oven and let it cool for a few minutes.
Dust with powdered sugar for added sweetness.
Slice and savor your Tula Tea Cake Supreme Pizza, a sweet and spiced dessert pizza inspired by the flavors of Tula tea cake!

Kulich Kiss Pizza

Ingredients:

- Pizza dough
- 1/4 cup cream cheese
- 1/4 cup kulich crumbs (Russian Easter bread), crumbled
- 1/4 cup honey
- 1/4 cup raisins
- 1/4 cup slivered almonds
- 1/4 teaspoon vanilla extract
- Powdered sugar (for dusting)

Instructions:

Preheat your oven according to the pizza dough instructions.
Roll out the pizza dough on a floured surface to your desired thickness.
In a bowl, mix together cream cheese, honey, and vanilla extract to create a creamy base.
Spread the creamy mixture evenly over the pizza dough.
Sprinkle crumbled kulich crumbs over the creamy base.
Evenly distribute raisins and slivered almonds over the toppings.
Bake in the preheated oven until the crust is golden, and the toppings are just heated through.
Remove from the oven and let it cool for a few minutes.
Dust with powdered sugar for added sweetness.
Slice and enjoy your Kulich Kiss Pizza, a delightful dessert pizza inspired by the flavors of Russian Easter bread, kulich!

Solyanka Splurge Pizza

Ingredients:

- Pizza dough
- 1/4 cup sour cream
- 1/4 cup tomato paste
- 1/4 cup dill pickles, sliced
- 1/4 cup cooked and sliced sausage (kielbasa or your choice)
- 1/4 cup cooked and sliced salami
- 1/4 cup cooked and sliced ham
- 1/4 cup cooked and sliced chicken
- 1/4 cup red onion, thinly sliced
- 1/4 cup green olives, sliced
- 1/4 cup capers
- 1/4 teaspoon black pepper
- Fresh dill, chopped (for garnish)

Instructions:

Preheat your oven according to the pizza dough instructions.
Roll out the pizza dough on a floured surface to your desired thickness.
In a bowl, mix together sour cream and tomato paste to create a saucy base.
Spread the saucy mixture evenly over the pizza dough.
Evenly distribute sliced dill pickles, cooked sausage, salami, ham, chicken, red onion, green olives, and capers over the saucy base.
Sprinkle black pepper over the toppings.
Bake in the preheated oven until the crust is golden, and the toppings are heated through.
Remove from the oven and let it cool for a few minutes.
Garnish with chopped fresh dill.
Slice and enjoy your Solyanka Splurge Pizza, a hearty and flavorful pizza inspired by the Russian soup, solyanka!

Sbiten Spice Pizza

Ingredients:

- Pizza dough
- 1/4 cup honey
- 1/4 cup sbiten spice syrup (a mix of water, honey, cloves, cinnamon, ginger, and other spices, boiled and strained)
- 1/4 cup cream cheese
- 1/4 cup chopped apples
- 1/4 cup chopped pears
- 1/4 cup dried cranberries
- 1/4 cup chopped nuts (walnuts, almonds)
- Powdered sugar (for dusting)

Instructions:

Preheat your oven according to the pizza dough instructions.
Roll out the pizza dough on a floured surface to your desired thickness.
In a bowl, mix together honey, sbiten spice syrup, and cream cheese to create a spiced, sweet base.
Spread the spiced cream cheese mixture evenly over the pizza dough.
Evenly distribute chopped apples, chopped pears, dried cranberries, and chopped nuts over the spiced base.
Bake in the preheated oven until the crust is golden, and the toppings are just heated through.
Remove from the oven and let it cool for a few minutes.
Dust with powdered sugar for added sweetness.
Slice and enjoy your Sbiten Spice Pizza, a unique and flavorful pizza inspired by the traditional Russian spiced drink, sbiten!

Zapekanka Zen Pizza

Ingredients:

- Pizza dough
- 1/2 cup tvorog (Russian cottage cheese)
- 1/4 cup sugar
- 1/4 cup sour cream
- 2 eggs
- 1/4 cup raisins
- 1/4 teaspoon vanilla extract
- 1/4 cup crushed graham crackers or biscuits
- 1/4 cup apricot jam
- Powdered sugar (for dusting)

Instructions:

Preheat your oven according to the pizza dough instructions.
Roll out the pizza dough on a floured surface to your desired thickness.
In a bowl, combine tvorog, sugar, sour cream, eggs, raisins, and vanilla extract.
Mix well to form a creamy mixture.
Spread the tvorog mixture evenly over the pizza dough.
Sprinkle crushed graham crackers or biscuits over the tvorog mixture.
Bake in the preheated oven until the crust is golden, and the tvorog mixture is set.
Remove from the oven and let it cool for a few minutes.
Heat apricot jam in a small saucepan until it becomes a liquid consistency.
Drizzle the liquid apricot jam over the pizza.
Dust with powdered sugar for added sweetness.
Slice and enjoy your Zapekanka Zen Pizza, a delightful dessert pizza inspired by the Russian baked tvorog dish, zapekanka!

Zharkoye Zest Pizza

Ingredients:

- Pizza dough
- 1/4 cup sour cream
- 1/4 cup tomato paste
- 1/4 cup cooked and diced beef
- 1/4 cup cooked and diced potatoes
- 1/4 cup cooked and diced carrots
- 1/4 cup cooked and diced peas
- 1/4 cup cooked and diced onions
- Salt and pepper to taste
- Fresh parsley, chopped (for garnish)

Instructions:

Preheat your oven according to the pizza dough instructions.
Roll out the pizza dough on a floured surface to your desired thickness.
In a bowl, mix together sour cream and tomato paste to create a saucy base.
Spread the saucy mixture evenly over the pizza dough.
Evenly distribute cooked and diced beef, potatoes, carrots, peas, and onions over the saucy base.
Season with salt and pepper to taste.
Bake in the preheated oven until the crust is golden, and the toppings are heated through.
Remove from the oven and let it cool for a few minutes.
Garnish with chopped fresh parsley.
Slice and enjoy your Zharkoye Zest Pizza, a flavorful and hearty pizza inspired by the Russian meat and vegetable stew, zharkoye!

Tvorog Toast Pizza

Ingredients:

- Pizza dough
- 1/2 cup tvorog (Russian cottage cheese)
- 1/4 cup honey
- 1/4 cup mixed berries (strawberries, blueberries, raspberries)
- 1/4 cup granola
- 1/4 teaspoon vanilla extract
- Powdered sugar (for dusting)

Instructions:

Preheat your oven according to the pizza dough instructions.
Roll out the pizza dough on a floured surface to your desired thickness.
In a bowl, mix together tvorog and honey to create a creamy mixture.
Spread the tvorog mixture evenly over the pizza dough.
Sprinkle mixed berries and granola over the tvorog mixture.
Drizzle vanilla extract over the toppings.
Bake in the preheated oven until the crust is golden, and the toppings are just heated through.
Remove from the oven and let it cool for a few minutes.
Dust with powdered sugar for added sweetness.
Slice and enjoy your Tvorog Toast Pizza, a delightful and healthy pizza inspired by the Russian cottage cheese, tvorog!

Ukha Utopia Pizza

Ingredients:

- Pizza dough
- 1/4 cup fish broth (ukha base)
- 1/4 cup sour cream
- 1/4 cup cooked and flaked white fish (cod, haddock)
- 1/4 cup potatoes, diced and boiled
- 1/4 cup carrots, diced and boiled
- 1/4 cup leeks, sliced
- 1/4 cup green peas, cooked
- 1/4 teaspoon dill, chopped
- Lemon wedges (for serving)

Instructions:

Preheat your oven according to the pizza dough instructions.
Roll out the pizza dough on a floured surface to your desired thickness.
In a bowl, mix together fish broth (ukha base) and sour cream to create a creamy fish sauce.
Spread the fish sauce evenly over the pizza dough.
Evenly distribute flaked white fish, diced and boiled potatoes, diced and boiled carrots, sliced leeks, and cooked green peas over the fish sauce.
Sprinkle chopped dill over the toppings.
Bake in the preheated oven until the crust is golden, and the toppings are heated through.
Remove from the oven and let it cool for a few minutes.
Serve with lemon wedges on the side for a citrusy touch.
Slice and enjoy your Ukha Utopia Pizza, a unique and savory pizza inspired by the Russian fish soup, ukha!

Holodets Happiness Pizza

Ingredients:

- Pizza dough
- 1/4 cup gelatinous holodets broth (strained meat jelly)
- 1/4 cup sour cream
- 1/4 cup cooked and shredded chicken
- 1/4 cup cooked and shredded beef
- 1/4 cup cooked and shredded pork
- 1/4 cup pickles, diced
- 1/4 cup red onion, thinly sliced
- 1/4 cup fresh parsley, chopped
- Salt and pepper to taste

Instructions:

Preheat your oven according to the pizza dough instructions.
Roll out the pizza dough on a floured surface to your desired thickness.
In a bowl, mix together holodets broth and sour cream to create a creamy base.
Spread the creamy mixture evenly over the pizza dough.
Evenly distribute shredded chicken, beef, and pork over the creamy base.
Scatter diced pickles and thinly sliced red onion over the toppings.
Season with salt and pepper to taste.
Bake in the preheated oven until the crust is golden, and the toppings are heated through.
Remove from the oven and let it cool for a few minutes.
Sprinkle chopped fresh parsley over the pizza.
Slice and enjoy your Holodets Happiness Pizza, a savory and hearty pizza inspired by the Russian meat jelly, holodets!

Kisel Kudos Pizza

Ingredients:

- Pizza dough
- 1/4 cup kisel sauce (fruit jelly sauce)
- 1/4 cup cream cheese
- 1/4 cup mixed berries (strawberries, blueberries, raspberries)
- 1/4 cup sliced peaches
- 1/4 cup kiwi, sliced
- 1/4 cup granola
- 1/4 cup mint leaves (for garnish)

Instructions:

Preheat your oven according to the pizza dough instructions.
Roll out the pizza dough on a floured surface to your desired thickness.
In a bowl, mix together kisel sauce and cream cheese to create a fruity, creamy base.
Spread the kisel cream cheese mixture evenly over the pizza dough.
Evenly distribute mixed berries, sliced peaches, and kiwi over the toppings.
Sprinkle granola over the pizza for added texture.
Bake in the preheated oven until the crust is golden, and the toppings are just heated through.
Remove from the oven and let it cool for a few minutes.
Garnish with fresh mint leaves.
Slice and enjoy your Kisel Kudos Pizza, a sweet and refreshing dessert pizza inspired by the Russian fruit jelly, kisel!

Paskha Perfection Pizza

Ingredients:

- Pizza dough
- 1/4 cup cream cheese
- 1/4 cup cottage cheese (tvorog)
- 1/4 cup powdered sugar
- 1/4 cup raisins
- 1/4 cup slivered almonds
- 1/4 cup candied orange peel, chopped
- 1/4 teaspoon vanilla extract
- 1/4 teaspoon orange zest
- Fresh berries (strawberries, blueberries) for garnish

Instructions:

Preheat your oven according to the pizza dough instructions.
Roll out the pizza dough on a floured surface to your desired thickness.
In a bowl, mix together cream cheese, cottage cheese (tvorog), powdered sugar, vanilla extract, and orange zest to create a creamy base.
Spread the creamy mixture evenly over the pizza dough.
Sprinkle raisins, slivered almonds, and chopped candied orange peel over the creamy base.
Bake in the preheated oven until the crust is golden, and the toppings are just heated through.
Remove from the oven and let it cool for a few minutes.
Garnish with fresh berries.
Slice and enjoy your Paskha Perfection Pizza, a delicious and festive dessert pizza inspired by the Russian Easter treat, paskha!

Pelmeni Party Pizza

Ingredients:

- Pizza dough
- 1/4 cup sour cream
- 1/4 cup cream cheese
- 1/4 cup cooked and drained pelmeni (Russian dumplings)
- 1/4 cup shredded mozzarella cheese
- 1/4 cup diced tomatoes
- 1/4 cup diced bell peppers (assorted colors)
- 1/4 cup sliced black olives
- 1/4 cup sliced green onions
- Salt and pepper to taste
- Fresh dill (for garnish)

Instructions:

Preheat your oven according to the pizza dough instructions.
Roll out the pizza dough on a floured surface to your desired thickness.
In a bowl, mix together sour cream and cream cheese to create a creamy base.
Spread the creamy mixture evenly over the pizza dough.
Evenly distribute cooked and drained pelmeni over the creamy base.
Sprinkle shredded mozzarella cheese over the pelmeni.
Scatter diced tomatoes, diced bell peppers, and sliced black olives over the toppings.
Season with salt and pepper to taste.
Bake in the preheated oven until the crust is golden, and the toppings are heated through.
Remove from the oven and let it cool for a few minutes.
Garnish with sliced green onions and fresh dill.
Slice and enjoy your Pelmeni Party Pizza, a unique and flavorful pizza inspired by the Russian dumplings, pelmeni!

Sbiten Sensation Pizza

Ingredients:

- Pizza dough
- 1/4 cup sbiten syrup (traditional Russian spiced honey drink)
- 1/4 cup cream cheese
- 1/4 cup cooked and shredded chicken
- 1/4 cup caramelized onions
- 1/4 cup roasted red peppers, sliced
- 1/4 cup feta cheese, crumbled
- 1/4 cup pine nuts
- Fresh dill (for garnish)

Instructions:

Preheat your oven according to the pizza dough instructions.
Roll out the pizza dough on a floured surface to your desired thickness.
In a bowl, mix together sbiten syrup and cream cheese to create a unique sauce.
Spread the sbiten cream cheese sauce evenly over the pizza dough.
Evenly distribute shredded chicken, caramelized onions, and sliced roasted red peppers over the sauce.
Sprinkle crumbled feta cheese over the toppings.
Scatter pine nuts over the pizza.
Bake in the preheated oven until the crust is golden, and the toppings are just heated through.
Remove from the oven and let it cool for a few minutes.
Garnish with fresh dill.
Slice and enjoy your Sbiten Sensation Pizza, a sweet and savory delight inspired by the traditional Russian spiced drink, sbiten!

Vareniki Velvet Pizza

Ingredients:

- Pizza dough
- 1/4 cup cream cheese
- 1/4 cup sour cream
- 1/4 cup strawberry or cherry jam
- 1/4 cup blueberries
- 1/4 cup powdered sugar (for dusting)
- Fresh mint leaves (for garnish)

Instructions:

Preheat your oven according to the pizza dough instructions.
Roll out the pizza dough on a floured surface to your desired thickness.
In a bowl, mix together cream cheese and sour cream to create a creamy base.
Spread the creamy mixture evenly over the pizza dough.
Dollop spoonfuls of strawberry or cherry jam across the creamy base.
Sprinkle blueberries over the jam.
Bake in the preheated oven until the crust is golden, and the toppings are just heated through.
Remove from the oven and let it cool for a few minutes.
Dust with powdered sugar for added sweetness.
Garnish with fresh mint leaves.
Slice and enjoy your Vareniki Velvet Pizza, a sweet and creamy dessert pizza inspired by the Russian dumplings, vareniki!

www.ingramcontent.com/pod-product-compliance
Lightning Source LLC
LaVergne TN
LVHW081502060526
838201LV00056BA/2889